Five Greyhound Peak

Ingrid Moberger Sanborn

The author retains sole copyright to this book,
including the contained original artwork.

Library of Congress Control Number: 2017901238

CreateSpace Independent Publishing Platform
North Charleston, SC

Acknowledgements

The author wishes to acknowledge a friend for his editing contributions to this work, Greta Shepard, for her formatting and assembly of this book, and her husband, Wayne, for his computer skills and perseverance.

The author's original illustrations were executed in Sumi-e watercolor on Japanese rice paper.

ASLAN

I am a light brindle dog, tan and black with deep chocolate eyes. At two years of age, I left the race-track for a greyhound rescue facility. They brought me muzzled, as if I were some kind of vicious dog. It was a relief to be out of a tiny track crate. They bathed us, gave us protective shots, and it was the first time I had decent food and an outdoor area to play in. But, oh, how I longed for a home of my own, with kind people to care for me and I for them.

One day a lady pulled up in a station wagon. I hoped she would notice me. There were many other greyhounds more beautiful than I. The rescue facility owner came to my kennel! She suggested that I might be a good match, but there was some kind of test for me. The rescue person led me to her cats, which were free to roam outside. I just sniffed them. I passed that test!

Then the lady took me for a walk. I was on my best behavior; I walked quietly by her side. I may not be one of the most beautiful greyhounds, but I am one of the smartest! Back at the rescue facility, the lady filled out papers and a soft nylon choke collar was put over my head with a lead line attached. I am out of here! The rescue person suggested borrowing a crate and muzzle because the lady had a Siamese cat. My new owner took me to the back of the station wagon, she opened the back, and I jumped in onto a soft, round dog bed! The crate and muzzle came too.

We came to a beautiful home, which was white with green shutters. There was a red barn and horse paddock, although I did not see any horses; there was a small fenced-in yard and back door to an ell of the house. We went inside. I was very nervous, but the lady, my new owner, was nervous too. She put the muzzle on me so I could meet Mocha, the Siamese cat. I fussed and shook my head. My owner took off the muzzle and just watched us. Soon Mocha and I were friends. I made short work of the crate too, so she returned it. Many greyhounds like a crate; they feel secure. I like my freedom. I slept quietly on the dog bed in my new owner's bedroom at night. This was heaven!

Most greyhounds have trouble adapting to food when they get a home. We ate such garbage at the track. We have allergies and sensitivities. It takes a while to find the right food. A raised water dish with clean water every day is wonderful.

At first, I just ran in tiny circles in the backyard, like I did at the track. My

owner did not like this behavior. She took me into the horse paddock; all the horses were gone. I began to see that I could run freely; it was fun.

A friend stopped by with her German shepherd dog. I ran circles around this dog until I was tired of this game. I held my paw up and howled. They thought I was hurt. My owner took me inside the house, and the shepherd and his owner went home. My owner examined my paw; there was nothing wrong with it. I had learned to do this at the track when I wanted to be left alone. My owner said, "You are a very clever dog!"

One day, my owner and her husband took me to the beach. I didn't like the sand, but they had a boat, so I had to get used to it. I learned very quickly to love the beach, swimming, and riding in the boat. I sat in the back of the boat, on the engine cover, with my nose in the air. My owners thought that I might fall out of the boat, but I never did.

When fall came, my owner and I were asked to come to the fair, so people could see greyhounds. I hoped that my friends at the rescue facility might also find homes. My owner and I walked around in a small ring. I let kids shake my paw. No one taught me this. I just did it for fun.

When we went home, I raced to my chair, curled up, and wouldn't move for the rest of the day. My owner said, "I see that this has bothered you.

It is too much like the race track. We will never go again". She is so perceptive of my needs and I of hers.

My owner's first grandchild came to visit. I loved him immediately and he loved me. He had brown hair and blue eyes and was very gentle. We ran together in the horse paddock. Of course, he could not keep up with me! We stopped playing and he gave me a dog bone.

Even though Mocha and I were friends, I was lonely for the company of another greyhound. My owner knew this. One day, we returned to the greyhound rescue facility. I became so frightened; I thought I had done something wrong and she was returning me. She told me to relax in the car and not to worry. Very soon, she came out with a female greyhound, called a red dog! There was another dog bed in the car that I had not noticed. Copper jumped into the car and home we went.

COPPER

I am a big, golden greyhound. I raced at the track and won many races. After four years of racing, I had had enough of track life.

I had a home for a short time, but the people couldn't keep me, so I was sent to the rescue facility.

One day, a woman came about adopting another greyhound. She had one greyhound and a Siamese cat. What do I care about chasing a cat? I don't want to chase anything any more. I was tested with cats at the rescue facility. I passed the test. Then, with a new collar and lead, the woman took me to a station wagon. Another greyhound was waiting for me inside it. Her name was Aslan. She told me about the cat named Mocha and what a great home she had.

We arrived home and I met Mocha, the cat. She and Aslan were friends and I wanted to be Mocha's friend, too.

I had not had to do stairs before, so Aslan had to show me how to go up and down. I took several stairs at a time on the way down.

Our owner took us for walks every day at the park. Aslan and I went on separate leads; soon our owner saw how perfectly we walked together.

She joined our leads together, with some space between them, of course. Aslan and I were very happy.

I had to get used to the boat, the beach, and the ocean. Aslan had learned to love it, she told me. I hated the greenhead flies and the boat rides. I would hide in the cabin in the front of the boat.

One day, we went in the boat to a sandbar that was surrounded by water at low tide. I watched as Aslan ran after birds and ate shells and crabs. She just never stopped running. I didn't care about running; I just wanted to be with my new owners. Soon, we all returned to the boat mooring. My owner said that we would be swimming to shore. Aslan jumped in the water and I reluctantly followed with my owner beside me. The next day, Aslan was sick from eating all the beach debris. She stayed all day in her chair because of sore muscles. I hoped she learned a lesson, but I doubted it.

When Aslan and I walked, if she saw some animal moving, she would shift into a beautiful high stepping trot with ears moving forward and back in a rhythmic motion. She had a hunting grace that I had never seen in any greyhound.

Mocha was very attached to Aslan. One day, Aslan got sick. Our walks

at the park got shorter and shorter. Mocha sat with Aslan on her dog bed. The day came when Aslan left Mocha and me. We were very lonely.

"The owner speaks: Aslan died of cancer at six years of age. It seemed too short a life for such a wonderful dog. My husband and I decided to adopt another greyhound; we would all be less lonely."

NINA

My name is Nina (hund) because my new owner is part Swedish. Hund means hound in Swedish. I am a dark brindle greyhound with beautiful golden eyes. I was not a good racer, so, at two years of age, the racetrack put me up for adoption. A woman and small boy took me, but they didn't keep me very long. The woman said that I bit the boy, but I would never intentionally do that. The woman took me to the greyhound rescue facility; I was there for a while. At least she did not return me to the track.

One day, a woman and small child came to see me. We walked around in a small space. The woman said that she did not think I would bite her grandson. Of course, I would not do that! I loved him right away and hoped that she would take me to her home. I passed the cat test and the lady decided to take me.

At her home was another greyhound named Copper. She was so happy to see me. There was also a cat named Mocha who was not in the least afraid of me. I liked her as well.

There were three grandchildren who visited often. My owner was a little wary that I might bite them. She watched me with them. The grand-

children were playing with me and getting me "wound up," when I started "cuffing." That is a nervous condition that I have. I kind of snap my jaw in excitement. When my owner saw this, she understood. She never let the grandchildren "wind me up" after that. We all played quietly.

I had another problem: I had seizures. I never understood what this was but my owner recognized it. The seizures happened when I had shots at the veterinary clinic. It was usually a result of the rabies shot. My owner and the veterinarian used many holistic procedures to lessen the effect of the rabies shot. It was scary for me and both of my owners.

My owner had a huge sandbox for the grandchildren. There were five grandchildren now. I always loved to be with them, but especially in the sandbox. They sat in the sandbox and told me to dig. I would make great holes and sand went everywhere. I loved to see the grandchildren laugh.

Copper and I walked at the park, but we had separate leads. We just didn't walk together well, as Copper had with Aslan. Copper told me all about her. I tried my best to be a good friend to Copper. We ran together in the horse paddock, but Copper was no longer interested in running. She would run a little and then just watch me as I raced around the paddock. I had never felt so free.

Then a very sad day arrived. Mocha had become such a good friend to both Copper and myself. She traveled everywhere around the neighborhood. No one could confine her. This day, she crossed our very busy street and was hit by a car. She died instantly. Copper and I whimpered.

"The owner speaks: We were all devastated by this loss. My husband and I decided that the best thing to do would be to go to the shelter and get another Siamese cat. We came home with two cats, a Snowshoe Siamese and a half-Himalayan, half-Siamese cat. The female Snowshoe Siamese we named Snowy. The male Himalayan/Siamese we named Leo, short for Leonardo. Because the greyhounds were used to cats, there was very little adjustment. All got along and life seemed good again.

Copper developed a very pronounced limp. We took her to the veterinarian, who diagnosed bone cancer in her left rear leg. We kept her until the pain was too much for all of us to bear. When we put her down we guessed her age to be about 10 years or more. Once again, we had lost a member of our family. We decided to adopt another greyhound for ourselves as well as for Nina, Snowy and Leo."

FLICKA

My name is Flicka, which in Swedish means little girl. My eyes are a rich deep brown. I am a white greyhound with a few brindle spots on my ears and a large spot on my back end. Everyone laughed about this big spot. I came to the greyhound rescue facility at two years of age. I was very sick, underweight with infected eyes and had Giardia, which comes from dirty water. The track was scary for me and I was abused. I would not run for them.

The same day that I arrived at the shelter, a woman came to see me. She told the rescue people that she must take me home. I was so sick she could not bear to leave me. The rescue people knew that she was a reliable greyhound owner. I hoped that she would be kind because I had only known misery in my two years of life. When I got scared, I would bite my tail until it bled.

The woman took me in a station wagon with a nice dog bed to curl up on. At their home were a greyhound named Nina and two cats, Leo and Snowy. I was so scared and sick I did not bother anyone. I just stayed on my dog bed.

My owner was so kind. She got me veterinarian care for my eyes and

medicine for Giardia. I had always been frightened, but with good food, clean water and friends I began to get better. It took two years to become physically healthy, but my fears never left me.

While I was still skinny and sick my owner took Nina and I to the State House in Boston where we were protesting dog racing. My owner thought that people should see my abused condition. The TV reporter came to see me. My owner told him to show my condition on TV so that people would vote against dog racing. They never showed me on TV. I don't know why.

Now with my owners and my greyhound Nina and cats Snowy and Leo, I became confident, but if a male person I didn't know came near me, I hid behind my owners for protection. Nina, the cats, and the grandchildren were a great comfort to me.

We traveled every summer to Cape Breton, Nova Scotia. The cats were in a red dog cage and Nina and I were on our dog beds in the station wagon. It is a long trip and we stayed one night in a motel on the way. We all loved it in Cape Breton. Nina didn't care much about Snowshoe Hares, red squirrels or birds, but I found that my hunting instincts had developed. I would give chase if I were not on a line. The cats and I watched

the wildlife through the screen doors. One red squirrel tormented us by first running to the front door and then to the back door. Our owners put a hook on each screen door. As we walked the road on lead lines, I loved to reach out and strip raspberries from the bushes that lined the road.

One fall at home in Massachusetts, Nina and I were running in the paddock. My owner said that I was even faster than Copper, who had been a top runner for four years at the race track. I ran much faster than Nina, but suddenly came to an abrupt stop when my leg went into a woodchuck hole. I could not move and was in shock. My owner picked me up and got me into the station wagon. At the veterinary clinic, they said that my leg was shattered. I stayed at the clinic overnight and next day was taken to a special clinic where my left front leg was amputated. This was a new kind of pain, but I was very brave because I had a wonderful family to go home to.

When I recovered, Nina and I had separate leads because my walk was more of a hop. I never complained through all the pain that I experienced. I learned to adapt, to balance on three legs. There were now six grandchildren and they called me "tripod." I didn't care because I loved them.

The next winter, Nina and I were running in the paddock. My owner noticed that I was running as fast on three legs as I had on four legs. She put a stop to my running in the paddock. She said it was too dangerous for me.

That same winter, Nina became sick with Lyme disease. I am white and it is easy to see deer ticks on my coat. Nina is a dark brindle and it is impossible to see ticks on her coat.

"The owner speaks: The next summer in Cape Breton, Nova Scotia, Nina died from complications due to Lyme disease. The cats and Flicka returned home with us to Massachusetts. My good friend was dying of cancer and could no longer take care of her greyhound. Her greyhound came to live with us and became a part of our family."

ROSIE

I am a very beautiful greyhound and I know it! I am a pink fawn color; I guess that is how I survived track life. I was a breeding dog. What the track people did not know was that I did not care about running and have very little hunting instincts.

I prefer not to talk about my past, except to say that I had spent time in a dog shelter with other breeds. A woman with two teenage boys took me from the shelter. I had spent a couple of years with them until they moved. The woman was going to take me back to the shelter. Instead, a woman with no children at home took me in. I was a good companion to her and she spoiled me. I slept on her bed at night and drank coffee out of her mug.

We walked every morning at the park with her friend, whose greyhound was named Flicka. She had only three legs. Sometimes I was pushy because I like to be first. Flicka's owner and my owner were great friends; they were both artists.

I thought I never had it so good, but one day everything changed. My owner had cancer and our walks got shorter and shorter. Soon, she brought me to Flicka's home. I thought I was just visiting, but my owner left me with Flicka. I only saw my owner one more time. Then I knew she had died. I had a new home with Flicka and the cats, Leo and Snowy. I don't bother the cats, but I like to do whatever I want to do.

My new owner was not like my former owner. I bit my new owner when she took a bone from me. I spent time in a big dog cage! This owner said that I must learn discipline. No more drinking coffee and sleeping on people beds for me. She let me understand that she was the pack leader.

In the small, fenced-in backyard, there was a bush called Shagbark Euonymous, which has razor sharp branches. I got a cornea tear in my eye when I put my head under this bush. It was so painful and I was not brave like Flicka. This happened to me twice, until my owner realized that I must never go near this bush.

In the summer, Flicka, Leo, Snowy, and I traveled to Cape Breton, Nova Scotia. I loved it there, just to be in the lush grass and hear the birds singing. Because Flicka could not go in the pontoon boat we stayed at our log home. We walked on the half-mile road to the top of the property. Flicka grabbed raspberries from the bushes along the side of the road. I did not want sharp brambles in my mouth. She wanted to chase snowshoe hares, but she was not let off her lead. In the fall, we returned to our

home in Massachusetts.

In the winter, Flicka and I played in the snow; our owner shoveled pathways for us to walk in. We had a good winter together.

Again, we traveled north to Cape Breton in June. Something was wrong with Flicka. When we got to the house, she just stayed on her dog bed. Cape Breton was the place that she loved the best. I could not understand her behavior. She had a funny bulge on her throat and our owner took her to the local veterinary office.

"The owner speaks: Flicka had developed cancer. We decided she had had enough pain in her life and did not need to suffer any more. The veterinarian put her down."

I knew what had happened to Flicka. My owner and I walked down to the beach and sat by the water. She began crying and I let out a piercing howl. I never realized how much I cared for this white greyhound. We sat and watched the waves breaking on the shore, feeling our loss. After a while, we went back to our log house. Snowy also seemed unwell.

After that, I got to go in the pontoon boat and I loved it. I sat on the cushioned seat like a queen. I missed Flicka but I loved these boat rides. On one boat trip, we stopped at a beach. There were eagles in the air

and hares on the ground. I was not let off the lead, but I had no interest in chasing the hares. When it was time to go, my owners put a towel around my middle and lifted me into the boat. We returned to the boat-lift and our log home. I hoped for more boat rides.

When we walked the road, I missed Flicka very much. Her funny twisted body, like an S-shape, and her hopping gate never seemed to keep her from wanting to chase a hare or a squirrel. We returned to Massachusetts in the fall.

"The owner speaks: Snowy was about sixteen years old. She was diagnosed with cancer. We kept her until she was in great pain; the veterinarian put her down. Now there were just Leo and Rosie. Leo looked for Snowy every day in the linen closet where she used to like to sleep."

Now there was only Leo and myself. We became great friends because we had lost Flicka and Snowy. Then, when winter came, Leo became very ill. He could not find his friend Snowy. Leo stopped eating and my owner took him to the veterinarian.

"The owner speaks: Leo was very ill and he was put down. He had spent his whole life with Snowy and his greyhound friends. Leo was about sixteen years old."

Now I was truly alone and missed my friends.

My owner and I went on election day to the voting polls. There was a referendum question to end dog racing in Massachusetts on the ballot. We walked and my owner talked to voters. They saw what a wonderful dog I was. We visited two towns and one city. A woman in the voting line asked my owner about adopting a greyhound. She had a cat at home. One veterinarian had told her not to have a greyhound with a cat, another veterinarian had said it was not a problem. I wished I could have told her how much I loved Leo and Snowy. Prospective greyhound owners need to be careful. A few greyhounds have such strong hunting instincts they might go after a cat. I was tired from meeting so many people; my owner saw this and took me home.

Some time later, my owner and I were walking in the park. In the distance I saw a woman with a brindle greyhound coming towards us. This was the woman that we had seen at the voting polls and that had asked about greyhounds with cats. This greyhound's name was Sweet Chris. Her Abyssinian cat was named Dinky. We all became good friends and Sweet Chris and I loved our walks together.

When summer came, my owners invited Sweet Chis, Dinky and their

owners to visit us at our home in Cape Breton. While they were there, a hurricane passed over Cape Breton. The winds were scary. After it passed by, we walked up the road and were grateful to see little damage. After they left, I was lonely again.

We returned to Massachusetts in the fall. I became quiet and took shorter and shorter walks. I just stayed on my bed most of the time.

"The owner speaks: Rosie died of kidney disease about age twelve. We did not know about her early life. She may have been older. With no animals, my husband and I traveled alone to Cape Breton the next summer. Because I had Lyme disease, I knew there will be no more greyhounds in our lives. We have been lucky to enjoy five greyhounds and three cats over the years. Greyhounds are wonderful and intuitive dogs. These animals lifted our spirits and lightened our hearts. They will never be forgotten."

CPSIA information can be obtained
at www.ICGtesting.com
Printed in the USA
LVHW070016150621
690236LV00013B/79